GREEN WAYS OF GETTING AROUND

CAREERS IN TRANSPORTATION

By Diane Dakers

CRABTREE
Publishing Company
www.crabtreebooks.com

Crabtree Publishing Company

Author: Diane Dakers
Publishing plan research and development:
  Sean Charlebois, Reagan Miller
  Crabtree Publishing Company
Editors: Mark Sachner, Molly Aloian
Proofreader: Crystal Sikkens
Editorial director: Kathy Middleton
Photo research: Ruth Owen
Designer: Westgrapix/Tammy West
Production coordinator: Margaret Amy Salter
Prepress technician: Margaret Amy Salter
Print coordinator: Katherine Berti
Production: Kim Richardson
Curriculum adviser: Suzy Gazlay, M.A.

Written, developed, and produced by Water Buffalo Books

Photographs and reproductions:
2010 Diamond Aircraft Industries GmbH: page 44.
Alamy: Randy Duchaine: page 34.
Nichole Blanchard: cover (bottom row left); page 53.
Alastair Callender: page 38.
Corbis: Christian Charisius: page 41 (top).
Coulomb Technologies Inc: cover (top row center right); page 1 (top right center); page 21.
FLPA: Rebecca Hosking: page 8; Fred Bavendam: page 28; John Eveson: page 33.
Getty Images: Jeff Kowalsky/Bloomberg: page 19.
Go Green Taxis: page 20.
Gini Holland: cover (2nd row right); page 14 (top).
Hornblower Cruises & Events All Rights Reserved: page 32.
Raymond W. Johnston: page 9.
Eric Knoshaug: cover (3rd row right); page 5 (bottom right).
Massachusetts Institute of Technology: cover (3rd row center); page 46 (right).
Pritesh Mody: page 46 (left).
Plastiki: Plastiki Crew: page 39; Patrick Riviere: page 40.
Peter Roy: page 35.
Science Photo Library: Peggy Greb (U.S. Department of Agriculture): page 13; Pasquale Sorrentino: page 14 (bottom); Carlos Dominguez: page 24; Simon Fraser: page 29; Hubert Raguet: page 45.
Shutterstock: cover (top row right); cover (3rd row left); cover (bottom row center); cover (bottom row right); page 1 (top right); pages 4–5 (background); page 4 (bottom center); page 4 (bottom right); page 5 (bottom left); page 5 (center); page 7 (center); pages 12–13 (background); page 15; pages 16–17 (all); pages 26–27; page 31; page 36; pages 42–43; pages 50–51; page 52 (all); page 55 (top); page 57 (all); page 58.
SkySails: page 37.
SmartBike: cover (top row center left); page 1 (top left center); page 56.
Solar Flight Inc: Dave Freund: page 47.
Solar Impulse: cover (top row left); page 1 (top left); page 48; page 49.
Transatlantic 21: page 40.
Val Waldron: page 25.
Wallenius Wilhelmsen Logistics: page 39 (top).
Jackie Weiler: cover (2nd row left); page 1 (center); page 23.
Wikipedia Creative Commons (public domain): cover (2nd row center); page 6 (bottom); page 10; page 11; page 12; page 22; page 30; page 41; page 55 (bottom).

Library and Archives Canada Cataloguing in Publication

Dakers, Diane
    Green ways of getting around : careers in transportation / Diane Dakers.

(Green-collar careers)
Includes index.
Issued also in electronic format.
ISBN 978-0-7787-4856-4 (bound).--ISBN 978-0-7787-4867-0 (pbk.)

    1. Transportation--Vocational guidance--Juvenile literature.
2. Transportation--Environmental aspects--Juvenile literature.
I. Title. II. Series: Green-collar careers

TA1160.D35 2011   j388.023   C2011-902564-7

Library of Congress Cataloging-in-Publication Data

Dakers, Diane.
 Green ways of getting around : careers in transportation / Diane Dakers.
    p. cm. -- (Green-collar careers)
 Includes index.
 ISBN 978-0-7787-4856-4 (reinforced library binding : alk. paper) --
ISBN 978-0-7787-4867-0 (pbk. : alk. paper) -- ISBN 978-1-4271-9720-7 (electronic pdf)
1. Transportation--Vocational guidance. 2. Transportation--Environmental aspects. 3. Sustainable development. I. Title. II. Series.

 TA1160.D35 2011
 388.023--dc22   2011013878

Crabtree Publishing Company
www.crabtreebooks.com   1-800-387-7650

Printed in China/082011/TM20110511

Published in Canada
Crabtree Publishing
616 Welland Ave.
St. Catharines, Ontario
L2M 5V6

Published in the United States
Crabtree Publishing
PMB 59051
350 Fifth Avenue, 59th Floor
New York, New York 10118

Published in the United Kingdom
Crabtree Publishing
Maritime House
Basin Road North, Hove
BN41 1WR

Published in Australia
Crabtree Publishing
3 Charles Street
Coburg North
VIC 305

CHAPTER 1

TRAINS, PLANES, AND AUTOMOBILES

Green Yacht Designer

Thousands of years ago, the only way for people to get around was to walk or run. That changed when the first-known wheeled vehicle was invented about 5,500 years ago. That invention, in turn, has evolved into all kinds of land transportation. These include carts, wagons, carriages, bicycles, automobiles, motorcycles, buses, and trains.

Boating has a similar history, beginning generations ago, when people first realized they could float on logs. That insight eventually led to rafts, canoes, rowboats, sailboats, motorboats, tankers, and cruise ships. As for flight, the legendary Wright brothers invented the first-ever successful flying machine in 1903. Now we have jets and helicopters that take us places Wilbur and Orville Wright could only have imagined!

Fuel Researcher

Green Car Inventor

Are you someone who likes to be on the go around your community, your city, your country— even the world? If so, a career in transportation could be for you! Exciting career options include:
• Airline or helicopter pilot
• Flight attendant
• Ferry captain
• Train engineer
• School bus driver
• Freighter deckhand
• Bicycle messenger
• Courier or delivery driver
• Long-distance trucker

Green City Planner

A Vast Network of Getting Around

Today, all these modes of transportation—on land, water, and in the air—form a vast, international network. This network moves people and goods pretty much anywhere they need to go, helping us deliver food and other necessities where they're needed. It also gives us greater freedom of movement, helps connect different cultures around the globe, and puts less-developed countries on the map. These systems require many people to help them run. They also require people to help research and develop vast energy sources to power them.

Our transportation systems include solar- and electric-powered cars, boats,

Below right: Eric Knoshaug in the lab

CAREER PROFILE

FUELING THE FUTURE: ALTERNATIVE FUEL RESEARCHER

My main role is to think of and develop ideas about switching from petroleum to renewable, sustainable resources, such as plants or algae. These resources help us meet our needs for liquid fuels—gasoline, diesel, and jet fuel.

My time is split between my office and lab. A typical day begins by answering my email and doing some paperwork. Next, I plan out my experiments for that day. Then I go to the lab and perform the experiments. Afterward, I look at the results to see if the experiments answered my questions as I thought they would, or if something unexpected happened!

Much of my work is with renewable fuel feedstocks. Feedstocks are raw materials, such as plants and algae, that can be used to fuel machines. By working on feedstocks I am helping reduce our use of oil. This should also help avoid the air and water pollution that goes with oil exploration, drilling, and use. What I love most about my work is that I am using my master's degree in microbiology to solve important problems in renewable fuels.

Eric Knoshaug
Senior Scientist
National Renewable Energy Laboratory
Golden, Colorado

WHAT ARE FOSSIL FUELS?

Fossil fuels started to develop millions of years ago as tiny marine plants and animals. Today, they come from deep beneath Earth's surface. When the marine organisms died all those years ago, they sank to the bottoms of rivers, lakes, and oceans. There, they were buried by sediment and eventually decomposed into pure carbon. Over vast periods of time, they have become converted to oil, coal, or gas.

and planes. They also include trains that are drawn along the tracks by magnetic fields and even "moving sidewalks" designed to let pedestrians take a load off when faced with long, hot walks.

Such developments have opened up doors to places where people could only dream of visiting. They have also helped us understand our obligation to travel in ways that help preserve the natural resources of our planet. These developments have improved our ability to promote the health and well-being of humans and other living things that depend on clean, green, and renewable resources. Because these resources are renewable, they do not damage the environment for future generations. We therefore call them *sustainable*. This means that they can be kept at a constant level. Where will our transportation lines take us next? Maybe that's something you'll discover if you choose a career in this field.

Why Go Green?

All this moving about via these many modes of transportation comes with a price. Right now, most vehicles on the road, rails, water, or in the sky, are

The effects of geography and weather can increase the impact of the burning of fossil fuels. Here, the smog hovering over Mexico City is a result not only of heavy industry and automotive traffic, but also of a landscape and climate conditions that help trap pollutants in the atmosphere just over the city.

powered by fossil fuels (gas, oil, and coal). When these fuels are burned, they release carbon dioxide, or CO_2, and other gases known as greenhouse gases into our air.

These gases have always been present in Earth's atmosphere, keeping our planet warm and able to support life. Today, the levels of these gases are at an all-time high, and they are still rising.

As the concentration of greenhouse gases increases, more and more of the Sun's heat is trapped within our atmosphere. Like the air in a greenhouse at a garden center, the temperature inside our planet-sized greenhouse is warmer than it would naturally be. This means that global temperatures are on the rise. Earth's temperature has risen about 1.33°F (0.74°C) in the past 100 years.

Scientists say the increase in greenhouse gases is the main cause of global climate change. With higher temperatures come extreme weather patterns, such as hurricanes, droughts, and floods. Rising temperatures also mean polar ice will continue to melt and glaciers will shrink. Water levels could rise, threatening low-lying communities and ecosystems across the planet. Plants and animals around the world have already begun to adapt, or move to new habitats, to survive.

Pollution Problems

Greenhouse gases don't just affect our weather systems. They also cause a kind of pollution called acid rain. When fossil fuels burn and produce CO_2, they also produce sulfur and nitrogen. These elements combine with water vapor, sunlight, and oxygen to create acids that

HOOKED ON FUEL FROM FOSSILS?

Fossil fuels took millions of years to develop, but now we are burning them so fast that supplies are running out. We can't rely on them forever, and we can't make more. Some scientists believe these fuel supplies will be used up within the next 100 years! Right now, though, fossil fuels are the most abundant, inexpensive, and convenient energy sources. Industrialized nations, such as those in North America and Europe, are hooked on them. The pie chart below shows the use of energy by different transportation modes in the United States in 2007.

PIPELINE 3.2%

RAIL 2.3%

WATER 5.6%

AIR 9.0%

MEDIUM/HEAVY TRUCKS 18.8%

LIGHT VEHICLES 60.4%

BUSES 0.7%

CAREER PROFILE

CHANGING DIRECTIONS: LOBBYIST IN SHIPPING INDUSTRY

I am in the marine transportation industry. This means that I work in transporting people and products by water. My career spans more than 30 years. Before I joined the Chamber of Marine Commerce, I was President and Chief Executive Officer (the person in charge) at Canada Steamship Lines. I worked there 23 years. During that time, I held several senior positions and gained expertise in all areas of the Canadian and U.S. shipping industries.

At the Chamber of Marine Commerce, my main role is to work with industries and governments to ensure a competitive, sustainable, and prosperous marine transportation industry.

What I enjoy most about my work is the variety! I have never done the same thing twice. The shipping industry is unique. It provides a window into so many other industries. These include agriculture, mining and steel, construction, and oil, to name a few. It is a truly global industry, and I have been lucky to travel to almost every corner of the world.

CONTINUED ON PAGE 9...

Raymond W. Johnston
President Chamber of Marine Commerce
Ottawa, Ontario

fall as rain or snow. These acids end up in rivers, lakes, streams, and soil. They harm plants and animals. They even damage buildings, historical monuments, and metal.

In the Western world, acid rain is on the decline because cars and industries are now required to filter harmful substances from exhaust systems. In Asia, however, where coal burning is more common, sulfur emissions—and acid rain—are still on the rise.

Another type of pollution that comes from some forms of transportation is noise pollution. Airplanes, freight trains, some trucks and motorcycles, and large ships are just plain loud. This can harm human hearing and disturb and frighten birds and animals in the wild.

Marine mammals, such as whales and dolphins, are particularly sensitive to sounds and vibrations that interrupt their undersea communications.

The dumping of garbage by the shipping industry has had a disastrous effect on marine life. Here, in Hawaii, a Pacific Green Turtle could suffocate from the plastic bag that it has mistaken for a jellyfish and tried to eat.

In addition, the international shipping industry has a history of dumping raw sewage, garbage, and wastewater into the oceans. All these forms of pollution are damaging to the plant and animal life of our marine environments.

New Directions

Economists predict that air travel, international shipping, and the number of cars on our roads will increase for years to come. As long as we rely on fossil fuels to power these vehicles, the threat of climate change and pollution is only going to get worse. Fortunately, though, scientists have realized this and are working on ways to reduce and maybe even stop our dependence on fossil fuels.

The transportation of people and products is the cause of almost one-third of greenhouse gas emissions. Making changes to the way we get around will almost certainly improve our air quality and help slow climate change.

Making Transportation Green—Work in Research and Development

Today, researchers, engineers, and environmentalists are hard at work developing new sources of energy to fuel our transportation needs. So far, they've had success with a number of alternatives. Maybe this is work you will continue, if you pursue a career in alternative fuel or transportation research!

CAREER PROFILE

CHANGING DIRECTIONS: LOBBYIST IN SHIPPING INDUSTRY

...CONTINUED FROM PAGE 8

My work has brought me in contact with people from all sorts of nationalities, cultures, and jobs. I have met with heads of state and traveled with former prime ministers. I have worked with executives from giant companies and dined with deckhands in the galleys of ships. I have had the chance to learn a business from the bottom up and inside out.

This industry is filled with opportunities and well-paying jobs both ashore and at sea. Are you someone who is looking for variety, exposure to global markets, and commercial challenges? Are you someone who has an interest in shaping the new environmental model for the shipping industry? If so, then this kind of work might be just right for you!

Raymond W. Johnston
President Chamber of Marine Commerce
Ottawa, Ontario

Raymond W. Johnston at the podium

The Sun is a brilliant source of energy. This solar-powered catamaran, called the *RA66 Helio*, collects energy from the Sun in solar cells that are arrayed in large panels. These cells convert that energy into electricity. The boat is shown here on Lake Constance, near its base in Germany.

Here are some areas that promise to offer plenty of chances to work in fields related to researching and producing sources of energy that are green, renewable, and therefore sustainable:

Solar energy. For millions of years, the Sun's rays have been supplying Earth with all the energy it needs to support life, grow food, and keep the planet warm. Today, researchers are discovering new ways to convert the Sun's energy into heat and electricity.

For transportation purposes, the Sun's energy is collected and converted to electricity by devices called photovoltaic cells or solar cells. The cells are grouped into panels to collect sunlight. The more power needed, the larger the solar panels. These panels are now being installed in the wings of airplanes and on the tops of boats to keep these vessels moving.

Sunlight is a clean, unlimited source of energy. The downside is that it only works during the daytime. Scientists are now developing batteries that can store enough solar energy to keep airplanes and other vehicles going all night.

Electric power. Electric-powered cars have been around for more than a century. Until recently, however, they haven't been reliable enough to be used on a regular basis. Today, researchers are focusing on electricity and battery power as serious alternatives to gasoline. Longer-lasting batteries and EV (electric vehicle) charging stations are in testing stages.

Electric-powered cars are quiet and clean, with no CO_2 production. The electricity that drives EVs is often produced by the burning of coal, however. This process releases greenhouse gases, which means that electric power isn't 100 percent clean. Also, electric-powered cars can't travel great distances between charges. Plenty of work remains to be done in researching and developing EVs that use sustainable energy to power vehicles over the long haul!

"Life really would be easier if fossil fuels such as oil and coal did not cause environmental damage or pose risks to life on our small planet. But this is the real world with real scientific evidence pointing to the urgent need to make changes in the way we live and get energy."

David Suzuki,
Environmentalist

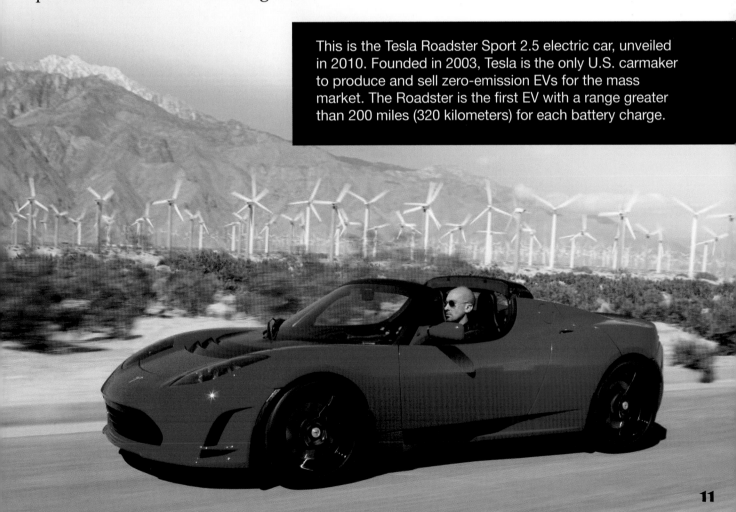

This is the Tesla Roadster Sport 2.5 electric car, unveiled in 2010. Founded in 2003, Tesla is the only U.S. carmaker to produce and sell zero-emission EVs for the mass market. The Roadster is the first EV with a range greater than 200 miles (320 kilometers) for each battery charge.

RUNNING GREEN

Walking is already the most eco-friendly way of getting from Point A to Point B. Now, thanks to new running shoe technology, walking and running are getting even greener.

The Green Silence, a high-performance running shoe, is made from recycled materials, soy-based inks, water-based adhesives, and eco-friendly rubber. More than 75 percent of the shoe's parts—laces, heel cups, and fabrics—are made from recycled materials.

The midsole (the cushion layer between the outer sole that touches the ground and the insole that touches your foot), is biodegradable. It contains an additive that helps the foam break down in 20 years instead of 1,000 years. The rubber of the outer sole is made from sand instead of petroleum. Making each shoe uses almost half the energy, and two cups (479 milliliters) less oil, than making a conventional running shoe.

Hybrid technology. A hybrid is any vehicle that combines two or more types of power. The most common hybrid today, when it comes to cars, is a gasoline-electric hybrid. This type of vehicle has a regular engine to burn gas and a battery to store electricity. Hybrids are quieter and more fuel efficient than gasoline-only cars. They also release fewer greenhouse gases into the air. On the downside, hybrids are more expensive than traditional automobiles. As a result, consumers have yet to fully embrace them. In 2009, in the United States, just 1.5 percent of cars on the road were hybrids.

Other hybrid crafts now under development are solar-electric aircraft and solar-wind-and-wave-powered boats.

Wind power. For centuries, wind has powered sailing ships, but its applications for other modes of transportation are, so far, limited. Again, much work remains to be done in finding ways of converting wind power to the operation of vehicles on land and in the air.

Introduced in Japan in 1997, the Toyota Prius was the world's first mass-produced hybrid car. It began selling worldwide in 2001.

Biofuels. Certain plants can be converted into alcohol and used as fuel through a process called fermentation. In this process, sugars and other substances found in plants are broken down by bacteria or other tiny organisms, giving off heat. One important product formed by this process is ethyl alcohol, or ethanol. Made from plants such as corn, potatoes, and sugar cane, ethanol is a renewable fuel source and releases less CO_2 than fossil fuels. For these reasons, it is already widely used as a fuel additive in regular gasoline. In some countries, some vehicles run on ethanol only. Other vehicles can switch back and forth between ethanol and gasoline.

The downside to ethanol as a fuel is that growing the plants to produce it requires pesticides, fertilizers, and a lot of water. It also requires large fields of agricultural land that could otherwise be used to grow food.

Biofuels used in automobiles don't work in airplane engines. For this reason, the aircraft industry is experimenting with its own biofuels. Right now, fuels made from algae and certain non-food, oil-rich plants, such as jatropha and camelina, are the most promising sources.

Fuel cells. A chemical reaction inside a hydrogen fuel cell mixes hydrogen and oxygen to produce electricity. In this process, the only byproduct is water! It sounds like the

Researchers harvest a giant reed plant *(Arundo donax)*. This plant is being tested as a source of ethanol for use as a biofuel. Large mats of these plants would be grown on lagoons of waste water, thus avoiding deforestation or using land needed for food crops.

15

This "alternatively empowered" truck is part of a tour encouraging bicycle use as a form of transportation. The truck uses biodiesel, which is made from animal fat, vegetable fat, and even used cooking oil. This fuel is designed to blend with ordinary diesel fuel. It is a renewable resource that releases fewer greenhouse gases than regular diesel.

A designer uses computer aided design (CAD) to create a new design for a hydrogen fuel cell scooter. CAD allows designs to be tested without spending the time and money needed to build a working model. This scooter will be powered by a hydrogen fuel cell rather than a standard engine.

perfect green solution for all our transportation needs. The problem is finding enough hydrogen to keep the engines running.

One way to capture hydrogen is to separate the hydrogen atoms out of hydrogen-rich compounds, such as natural gas. This process takes a lot of energy, however, and can produce harmful byproducts. These include carbon monoxide and carbon dioxide, although the amount of CO_2 produced is much less than would be produced by burning gasoline.

Compressed Natural Gas (CNG). Used in modified gasoline engines, CNG is natural gas that has been super-compressed. This makes it about 100 times more concentrated than it is in its natural state. That means it takes up about 1/100 of the space it would in its natural state. CNG produces fewer greenhouse gas emissions than regular gasoline. It is a sealed fuel system. This means that there is no threat of spills that might contaminate the ground and water beneath the ground or in nearby rivers or lakes. Also, a CNG car engine has lower maintenance costs than a traditional engine.

On the other hand, CNG tanks are big and heavy, and a fill-up won't take you as far as a tank of gasoline. In Pakistan, India, and other parts of the world, CNG cars are very popular. They have yet to make a big splash in the United States.

Even with "carpool" lanes for vehicles with two or more passengers, traffic on this Los Angeles freeway is clogged as far as the eye can see. The emissions produced by these cars will eventually settle into a cloud of smog over L.A.

What's in the Cards for You?

Do you foresee developing these or other undiscovered energy sources in your future? Perhaps researching new, green technologies will be your passion. Or maybe you're excited about operating vehicles that travel over land, on water, or in the air.

Whichever direction you take, career opportunities in transportation are as wide as the skies—and growing!

"Green renewable energy transportation technology has a huge potential to reduce our air, water, and land pollution. By pursuing a career in this field, you are helping to solve one of the most vexing problems mankind will encounter— that of our energy use. Green technologies have a bright future!"

Eric Knoshaug,
Senior Scientist,
U.S. National Renewable
Energy Laboratory,
Golden, Colorado

The wheels of the bus go round and round. So do the wheels of cars, trucks, trains, motorcycles, scooters, bicycles, skateboards, rickshaws, wagons, and Rollerblades. Contact between wheels and the ground is a dynamic feature of just about every form of land transportation, except, of course, the most eco-friendly way of getting around: walking.

In the City, Around the Town

Are you someone who likes looking through windows, taking in the world around you, and observing your surroundings as you travel through life? If so, you might consider a career in ground transportation.

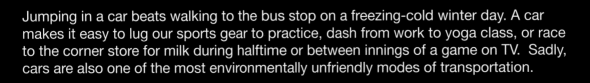

Jumping in a car beats walking to the bus stop on a freezing-cold winter day. A car makes it easy to lug our sports gear to practice, dash from work to yoga class, or race to the corner store for milk during halftime or between innings of a game on TV. Sadly, cars are also one of the most environmentally unfriendly modes of transportation.

You could help kids get to school on time as a school bus driver, deliver important packages as a bicycle messenger, or zip through the countryside in the driver's seat of a high-speed train. All of these jobs would also give you a chance to help the environment by providing clean, efficient ways of getting people and products where they need to go.

If you're outgoing and like meeting people who are on the go, perhaps becoming a ticket taker or a service attendant on a train, a taxi driver or dispatcher, or a city bus operator would suit you. For those budding inventors, scientists, and researchers out there, new energy sources, eco-friendly transportation technologies, and fuel-efficient vehicle designs are just waiting to be discovered.

A Quick Fix

When it comes to transportation, we love our cars. Some people even say our society is addicted to the automobile. Having a car— or two—makes for a convenient, quick, and comfortable way to get around. It gives us independence to go where we want, when we want.

WHAT GOES AROUND ...

What is round, essential to automobiles, and black—but not the least bit "green"? If you answered "tires," you are correct. Right now, it takes about seven gallons (26.5 liters) of oil to produce enough synthetic (artificial) rubber to make one tire. Every year, companies such as Bridgestone, Michelin, and Goodyear produce hundreds of millions of tires. That adds up to a lot of oil!

What if you could produce synthetic rubber (also called isoprene) from plants and reduce the use of fossil fuels? That's exactly what Goodyear and Genecor, a biotechnology company in Denmark, asked themselves. They've just come up with the answer.

The two companies have developed a process that uses bacteria to turn sugars from plants (such as sugar cane, corn, and certain grasses) into a type of synthetic rubber. The first tires made out of this substance, called bio-isoprene, are expected to be available to the public by 2015.

A magnetic levitation (Maglev) train cruising near Shanghai, China. Using a magnetic force field to suspend the cars and propel them over a monorail, the train is faster, quieter, smoother, and more energy efficient than conventional trains. The Maglev has also raised some concerns that researchers are investigating regarding the safety of the magnetic field and the train's reliability at slower speeds.

TOP-TEN AUTOMOBILE USERS

RANK	COUNTRY	MOTOR VEHICLES per 1,000 people
1	United States	765
2	Luxembourg	697 (2008 data)
3	Iceland	658
4	Australia	619
5	Puerto Rico	617 (2004 data)
6	Italy	571 (2008 data)
7	Canada	563
8	New Zealand	560
9	Austria	558
10	Germany	558

This chart shows the world's ten top users of the automobile, ranked according to the number of vehicles for every 1,000 people.

It's no wonder we can't seem to live without our personal vehicles—and the world's reliance on them is growing.

In the United States, the number of fuel-powered vehicles has increased almost every year since the 1960s. Right now, there are about 250 million cars, trucks, SUVs, motorcycles, and other passenger vehicles on U.S. roads. That works out to about 765 vehicles per 1,000 people. This makes the United States the world's top user of the automobile. In addition to the United States proper, Puerto Rico adds another 617 cars per 1,000 people. This makes the island territory number 5 on the list. Canada is number 7 on the list, with 563 cars per 1,000 people. Australia is number 4, with 619 cars per 1,000 people. The UK ranks 22nd, with 458 vehicles per 1,000 people.

It's clear we're not ready to give up our cars. But we can't ignore the fact that they are responsible for 80 percent of transportation energy consumption and 13 percent of transportation emissions. From an environmental point of view, cars are among the worst things on wheels.

BRING IN THE NOISE

Here's a job you've probably never heard of—sound designer for electric cars.

One of the great things about electric vehicles (EVs) is that they don't add to the noise pollution on our streets. That's also a downside. EVs are so silent that they can be dangerous to hearing and visually impaired pedestrians, children, and cyclists. They can also pose a danger to anyone who doesn't look both ways before crossing the street.

The challenge is to find a sound that pedestrians can hear and easily identify. It must also be a sound that doesn't annoy the neighbors or the car's driver. Nissan, for example, has been researching appropriate sounds for its electric car, the Leaf, since 2007.

Company researchers have worked with a Hollywood sound design company and acoustic psychologists (who give advice on how people respond to various sounds) to come up with about 100 different sounds. They tried these out with real people on the streets of Japan and the United States and narrowed the sounds down to one.

Knowing this, and knowing that we, as a society, are not ready to go car-free, some automobile designers and manufacturers are hard at work creating vehicles that are more eco-friendly. If this is something you'd like to help with, you might choose a career as an automotive engineer. You might also want to look at becoming an alternative-fuel researcher. Or you might want to become a lobbyist working to convince politicians to pass laws to promote green, sustainable transportation.

Cars That Care

Leading the charge in the Earth-friendly automotive movement is an assortment of cars that rely on energy sources other than fossil fuels. These include electric cars, hybrid taxicabs, compressed natural gas (CNG) automobiles, and biofuel-powered vehicles. Also at the top of the list of clean vehicles are buses powered by hydrogen fuel cells. These vehicles mix hydrogen and oxygen to create electricity.

QUALITIES NEEDED TO DO GREEN AUTOMOTIVE RESEARCH

Alternative fuel researcher:

• Organized and attentive to details

• Good observation skills and reliable report-writing skills

• A questioning mind, a desire to discover new and interesting things

• Creative, open-minded, a problem-solver who likes coming up with (and carrying out) experiments or tests

Automotive engineer:

• All of the above, plus these:

• A love of cars, automotive technology, and designing or redesigning vehicles

• An understanding of mechanics, computer systems, and the technology of vehicles

• The ability to work as part of a team, or lead a team, to solve mechanical, electronic, aerodynamic, emission, or safety problems

Workers assemble a Ford Transit Connect Electric van in Livonia, Michigan. The first of these all-electric vans were delivered to dealerships to be sold in 2010.

HYBRID TAXI TRAILBLAZING

On November 1, 2000, a Vancouver, British Columbia, taxi driver traded his Toyota Camry cab for a 2001 Toyota Prius. In doing so, Andrew Grant became the world's first cabbie to drive a hybrid cab. Two years and 205,000 miles (330,000 km) later, Andrew traded in that first car for a 2003 model. He traded up once more to a 2004 Prius before retiring from the taxi business after 25 years. In 2004, the first hybrid cab took to the streets in London, UK. In the following year, San Francisco and New York City became the first U.S. cities to introduce hybrid taxis.

One of the leaders in eco-friendly transportation is the Canadian resort town of Whistler, British Columbia. In 2010, the town, located 70 miles (112 km) north of Vancouver, purchased 20 hydrogen fuel cell buses. That makes it the largest fuel cell bus fleet in the world. The town is also home to the largest hydrogen cell fueling station in the world.

In San Francisco, California, the taxi industry is doing its share, boasting the largest green fleet in the United States. As of spring 2010, almost 60 percent of cabs on San Francisco roads were either hybrid or compressed natural gas vehicles. So far, introducing green cabs into the fleet has reduced fuel consumption by 2.9 million gallons (11 million liters) a year. That's equivalent to taking 4,700 gasoline-fueled cars off the road!

Michael Hatter and Mark John, directors of Go Green Taxis in South Oxfordshire, United Kingdom, stand beside one of their fleet of Prius hybrid taxis. Their company Web site proudly proclaims their use of green taxis "that won't cost the earth." They also run a paperless office, and even the lettering on their cabs is done using the UK's first environmentally friendly print system! Might starting an eco-friendly taxi or delivery

Going the Distance in EVs

A number of auto manufacturers are now making electric vehicles (EVs) the focus of their research and development. One of the main problems researchers must solve is how to keep these cars charged up over long distances.

Right now, an EV can't travel more than 100 to 200 miles (161 to 322 km) without a battery charge. But progress is being made.

In 2009, EV manufacturer Tesla Motors partnered with solar designer SolarCity to create the world's first charging corridor. This is a series of five charging stations located between San Francisco and Los Angeles. The stations, two of which are solar powered, are 70 to 100 miles (113 to 161 km) apart. This means that EV drivers can make the 382-mile (615-km) journey with just one or two charging stops

"The electric car is not just a pipe dream or a scene from *The Jetsons*. It is here, and it is here right now."

New York Mayor
Michael Bloomberg

This EV charging station in Madison, Wisconsin, is part of the station installation program called ChargePoint America.

EVs: A BRIEF HISTORY

During the 1800s, a variety of U.S. and European inventors tried out several small electric motors and model electric cars. The first full-size electric automobile was actually a simple electrified carriage invented in Scotland in 1832. By 1900, the electric car was the most popular car on the road. It was more common than steam- and gasoline-powered types. Electric cars were quiet and offered a smooth ride. They also didn't require hand cranking to start or gear shifting while driving, as did the gasoline-powered cars. Even though electric cars were available into the 1920s, their popularity began to decline around 1912, when oil became plentiful. That was also when Henry Ford was mass-producing affordable gas-powered cars and the hand crank was replaced with an electric starter system.

In the mid-1960s, the idea of electric vehicles (EVs) resurfaced during political discussions about reducing air pollution. A decade later, when oil prices skyrocketed, EVs were again in the spotlight. Over the next 30 years, a number of EV incentive programs were set up, but they were scrapped before they took off.

By 2009, EVs were back. They owed their return in part to the rising price of oil and in part to public demand. Government incentives have also led some car companies to build electric and hybrid cars.

WHY TAKE TRANSIT?

- Without public transit, far more cars would be on the road. These cars would use an additional 4.2 billion gallons (15.9 billion liters) of gasoline in the United States every year.

- Families that live near public transit drive an average of 4,400 fewer miles (7,000 fewer km) a year than those without access to public transit.

- By taking transit instead of driving to work, a commuter can reduce his or her carbon footprint (CO_2 emissions) by 10 to 30 percent.

- One full commuter train can take up to 800 cars off the road.

Commuters read their morning newspapers on the New York City subway. People board public transit vehicles 35 million times each weekday in the United States. Public transportation takes cars off the road and helps relieve traffic congestion.

along the way. Plugging in is free.

Meanwhile, Coulomb Technologies, Inc., a company that sets up electric vehicle charging stations, is in the process of installing 5,000 EV charging stations in nine regions of the United States by fall 2011. The program is called ChargePoint America. It is a partnership between Coulomb and three automakers—Ford, Chevrolet, and Smart USA. These companies are committed to designing and manufacturing EVs.

Designing and building alternative-fuel vehicles and researching new fuel sources and technologies are growing fields right now. Maybe these are areas you'd like to charge into as you consider your future career!

Go Public, Go Green

Public transportation systems include buses, subways, commuter trains, and conventional railroads. They also include light rail, high-speed trains, monorails, streetcars, cable cars, trolleys, and ferries. Just imagine all the different jobs associated with public transportation!

More than 380,000 people work in public transit systems in the United States. These people operate, maintain, and manage all these forms of transportation. Some of the jobs in public transportation are obvious. These include being a bus or train driver, a mechanic, or a ticket taker. Other jobs aren't so apparent to the public that uses the system.

Marketing professionals come up with campaigns, brochures, and advertisements to encourage passengers to use transit services. Then there are the folks who answer the phones when you call for information about schedules, routes, and fares.

On the more technical side are IT (information technology) people who deal with complex computer systems that keep buses and trains running on schedule. In addition, running a transportation system needs planners to prepare for future growth. These people also organize schedules and plan the complicated web of transit routes that we take for granted every time we get on a bus or train.

Riding the Rails

When it comes to traveling by rail, people and products may be sent on passenger, freight, commuter, long-haul, or sightseeing trains. These trains get their energy in a variety of ways—from electricity, diesel fuel, and magnetic levitation (Maglev). Some get their energy from hybrid combinations of rechargeable energy storage systems and fuels based on diesel, hydrogen, liquid gas, or steam. High-speed rail gets people where they are going faster. It also makes more efficient use of fuel at higher speeds. As with other

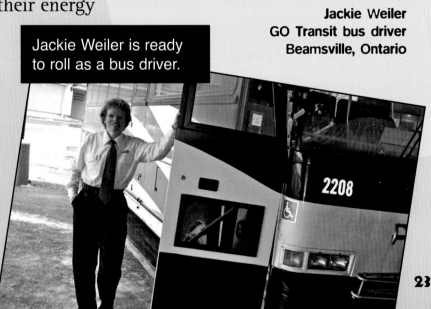

Jackie Weiler is ready to roll as a bus driver.

CAREER PROFILE

MISSION CONTROL: SKYTRAIN CONTROL CENTER SUPERVISOR

I work in the Control Center of the oldest and one of the longest fully automated "electric train sets" in the world. It's located in Vancouver, British Columbia, and it's called SkyTrain.

What makes SkyTrain different than a lot of other rapid transit systems is that it's "driverless." This means that, with some exceptions, you won't find people in the driver's seat of our trains. Instead, there are people (like my crew and me) in a Control Center who control the computers that drive the trains.

The Control Center has dozens of computer screens and television monitors to help us keep an eye on the entire SkyTrain system. We can see where all our trains are and where we might need to add a train to help move passengers off a crowded platform. We can also keep an eye on what's happening in our rail yard.

CONTINUED ON PAGE 25...

Val Waldron
Control Center Supervisor
British Columbia Rapid
Transit Company (SkyTrain)
Burnaby, British Columbia

land vehicles, the less a train depends on fossil-based fuel, the cleaner and more environmentally friendly it is.

Working the Rails

Today, rail travel is considered one of the most environmentally friendly ways of getting around. Regardless of how energy-efficient any given train is, most railroads need the same kinds of employees: engineers to operate trains, baggage handlers to load and unload luggage, and conductors to take tickets and greet travelers.

Freight trains need cargo handlers to load and unload goods by hand, by cart, and by crane.

A maintenance worker repairs railroad tracks in England as a train rushes past behind him.

Not all railroad workers ride the rails. Inspectors and maintenance people monitor and repair fences, tracks, and bridges. They take care of signals and lights at rail crossings and embankments beside the tracks.

In the rail yard, yardmasters make sure trains are loaded, arrange to move train cars around the yard, and organize trains as they arrive and depart. Meanwhile, dispatchers organize and direct train traffic, making sure the trains run safely and on schedule.

All you really need to work in the railroad industry is a true love of trains!

From her desk at the Control Center, Val Waldron helps more than 350,000 SkyTrain passengers reach their destinations daily.

CAREER PROFILE

MISSION CONTROL: SKYTRAIN CONTROL CENTER SUPERVISOR

...CONTINUED FROM PAGE 24

My first job at SkyTrain was as a SkyTrain attendant. SkyTrain attendants drive the SkyTrains when there is a problem. They also provide passengers with travel information and first aid. After ten years in that position, I was accepted into the SkyTrain Control Center training program. Then I worked as a Control Operator for about eight years before becoming a Control Center Supervisor.

A highlight for me in this job was being part of the success of the Vancouver 2010 Olympic and Paralympic Winter Games. For the 17 days of Games in February 2010, our two SkyTrain lines carried 64 percent more people than normal. That added up to nearly 400,000 passengers per day, without one major incident!

I feel very lucky to do the kind of work I do. It's an extraordinary job with a lot of responsibility. But if I can do it, so can you!

Val Waldron
Control Center Supervisor
British Columbia Rapid
Transit Company (SkyTrain)
Burnaby, British Columbia

CHAPTER 3

ANCHORS AWEIGH— WATER TRAVEL

You can sail a sailboat, paddle a canoe, or row a boat with little environmental damage. But other forms of ocean, lake, and river transportation aren't necessarily so eco-friendly. Luckily, many people are working hard to change that right now. Will you be one of those people whose career is geared to greening up the deep blue sea?

Floating through Life

How many different kinds of watercraft can you name? There are dozens. They range from the smallest raft or fishing boat to the largest oil tanker or container ship.

Top to bottom: a container ship loaded with freight for international shipping, kayaks for rent, and a Coast Guard ship rushing to someone's aid.
Right: a luxury cruise ship

If you love being on the water, any of these vessels could potentially provide a career for you. You might be the captain in charge of a ferry or tanker. You might choose to fish for a living or operate a canoe and kayak rental shop. Maybe you'd like to work on a Coast Guard ship rescuing people on the high seas.

Those who love the water but prefer working on land also have plenty of jobs to choose from. Some, such as doing research and development of more efficient ship designs and fuels, have a green focus. But there are also plenty of careers that simply support boating of any sort. These include working in ports and marinas, boat building, boat sales, and boat mechanics. There is also plenty of work to be done in the administration office of a cruise ship line, ferry terminal, or international shipping organization.

It's a Dirty Job

Just as trucks, cars, and airplanes have a dirty downside, so do marine vessels. Like most other vehicles, ships rely on fossil fuels for their power. As we've already seen, that means they release harmful greenhouse gases into the atmosphere.

"If global shipping were a country, it would be the sixth largest producer of greenhouse gas emissions."

Ellycia Harrould-Kolieb, *Shipping Impacts on Climate: A Source with Solutions* (Washington, D.C.: Oceana, 2008)

A cruise ship sits docked at a port of call. Of the four vessels shown here, cruise ships have the worst record when it comes to keeping oceans free of contaminants and waste. Fortunately, many cruise lines have joined the Cruise Lines International Association. These lines have agreed to abide by the organization's strict standards. Other lines have gone a step farther and developed their own initiatives for clean standards.

BLACK CARBON

Ship fuel is the dirtiest fuel around. In fact, it is so unrefined that, at room temperature, you can walk on it! Because of that, it doesn't just release greenhouse gases when it burns. It also spews soot—or black carbon—out of a ship's smokestacks. That soot forms clouds that can travel great distances. These clouds carry black carbon deposits onto Arctic snow and ice, into the water, and into the lungs of people. Believe it or not, about 60,000 people die every year worldwide from lung cancer or other heart and lung disorders directly related to the black carbon produced by ships.

Shipping is responsible for three percent of the world's CO_2 emissions. That may not sound like a lot, but it's equivalent to the amount of CO_2 produced by the whole country of Japan. It's as much pollution as is produced by 205 million cars. That's more cars than what exists in the entire United States.

The CO_2 from shipping directly affects our oceans. For one thing, it causes them to become warmer and more acidic. That, in turn, hurts coral reefs, shellfish, and other marine life. Rises in ocean temperatures also cause ice to melt in the polar regions. When ice caps melt, sea levels rise and coastal ecosystems are forever changed.

Waterborne Invaders

It's not just greenhouse gases we have to worry about when it comes to floating vessels. Ships dump garbage and sewage at sea. Along with oil and chemical leaks, this disrupts and harms marine life.

Coral reefs in 90 countries around the world are regularly damaged by cruise ship anchors and sewage. The reefs are also harmed by passengers breaking off pieces of coral for souvenirs and by locals who harvest it to sell to cruise passengers. The bleached area on this Staghorn Coral colony in Kimbe Bay, Papua New Guinea, was caused by contaminants introduced by human sources.

Other problems, such as biofouling and the introduction of invasive species, are also very serious concerns associated with shipping and boating. Biofouling happens when aquatic plant or animal life clings to the surface of a ship. Among the most common types of animals found on ship surfaces are barnacles. These organisms can contribute to the rusting and deterioration of the ship's surface. If they build up in great enough numbers, they can also affect the performance of the ship at sea. The changes in the surface of the ship can make it harder to navigate and maneuver. They can also slow the ship down. This causes it to use more fuel, thereby increasing the number of pollutants created by burning ship fuel.

The introduction of invasive species occurs when a plant or animal species is brought into an environment to which it is not native. When these organisms move into a new area,

WHAT DOES A BIOFUEL RESEARCHER DO?

If you were a biofuel researcher, you might work in a lab, in the field, or a bit of both. In the field, you would collect samples of, say, plants or algae that might be converted to a fuel source. That might mean splashing through ponds and rivers. Or it might mean tramping through an agricultural field to harvest the plants needed. This fieldwork could take you all over the area where you live, or even farther. It all depends on where the plants are growing.

In the lab, you would do a number of tests and experiments, such as analyzing the exact composition of a particular plant. Your work might involve figuring out which plants to use as feedstocks. It might also include tests to determine which types of algae are most promising for growing new strains. No matter what you do in this field, you would be contributing to greening the field of transportation.

A lab researcher examnines barnacles that have become attached to a piece of wood. This researcher is part of a program aiming to develop a coating to counteract the natural adhesive that allows barnacles, a major source of biofouling, to cling to rocks and boats.

they compete with the native species and can take over. They may even cause native species to disappear from the area entirely. A prime example of a ship-borne invasive species is the zebra mussel. The larvae, or young, of the mussel may attach themselves to boats. Zebra mussels have invaded and caused serious damage in the Great Lakes region in North America. They can also spread via pleasure craft towed from lake to lake.

Fortunately, organizations such as the United Nations' International Maritime Organization exist to help our oceans and waterways stay green. They have implemented regulations and standards that member countries agree to follow. They also continually research the impacts of shipping and boating on our environment, and they ensure the safety of our waters.

Loading cars and passengers onto a Washington State ferry. Washington State Ferries is the busiest and largest U.S. ferry system. This system has 23 vessels that carry up to 2,500 passengers and 200 vehicles each. Each year, the system transports 10 million vehicles and 23 million passengers. Tip to job seekers: It takes more than 1,500 people to keep the system moving efficiently!

A Future in Ferrying?

Ferries carry people, cars, and sometimes cargo across bodies of water. They may travel across small rivers and inlets or wide sections of ocean and large inland lakes, such as the Great Lakes. Sometimes they are part of road systems or even municipal transit systems.

The busiest ferry corridor in the world is the English Channel, with dozens of ferries traveling between England and France.

Another busy ferry service—and one of the best known—is New York City's Staten Island Ferry. This system operates a fleet of nine vessels. They provide service to over 20 million passengers a year across New York Bay between Lower Manhattan and Staten Island.

In Canada, BC Ferries operates one of the largest ferry services in the world. The system has 36 vessels transporting people and vehicles on 25 different routes to 47 terminals in British Columbia. In 2009, the system carried 8.3 million vehicles and 21 million passengers. About 4,500 employees work for BC Ferries. Maybe you'd like to make that 4,501!

FERRY FUEL FOR TOMORROW

Washington State Ferries and BC Ferries both operate in the region of the United States and Canada known as the Pacific Northwest. These systems are leaders in the use of more efficient fuels. Both have experimented in recent years with biofuels.

In 2010, BC Ferries switched 31 of its 36 ships to a 5 percent canola-based biofuel-diesel blend. This blend emits fewer greenhouse gases and less soot than conventional fossil-based fuels.

In 2008, Washington State Ferries tested a 20 percent biofuel-diesel blend on three ships. Researchers found that the fuel worked well. The blend significantly reduced the emission of harmful substances into the atmosphere. On the downside, though, the new fuel produced a lot of sludge that clogged the engines. Researchers have gone back to the drawing board to find a fix for that problem.

Shown here: New York's Staten Island Ferry terminal (below) and one of its boats (left). The ferry is used to carry automobiles and other vehicles between Manhattan and Staten Island. That service was suspended in the wake of the terrorist attacks of September 11, 2001.

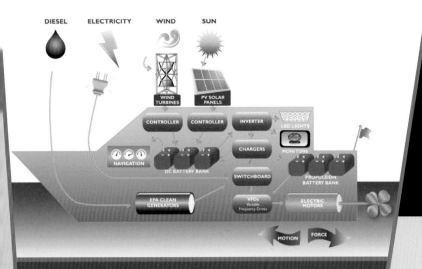

DIESEL   ELECTRICITY   WIND   SUN

WIND TURBINES   PV SOLAR PANELS

CONTROLLER   CONTROLLER   INVERTER   LED LIGHTS

CHARGERS   MONITORS

NAVIGATION

DC BATTERY BANK   SWITCHBOARD   PROPULSION BATTERY BANK

EPA CLEAN GENERATORS   VFDs Variable Frequency Drives   ELECTRIC MOTORS

MOTION   FORCE

This diagram of the Hornblower Hybrid illustrates the ferry's use of four different energy sources—diesel, electricity, wind, and solar. Working together, these energy sources make the ship a cleaner, more fuel-efficient vessel.

HERE COMES THE SUN

The Solar Shuttle is a type of sun-powered ferry. It has been operating in Germany and Switzerland since 2000 and in England since 2006. The Hamburg (Germany) Solar Shuttle is the largest of the three passenger ferries made by a British company called SolarLab. It carries up to 120 passengers along the Alster River into the Hamburg Harbor at a maximum speed of about nine miles per hour (15 km/h).

Another sun-kissed ferry is powered by the Solar Sail, a fixed wing that captures solar and wind energy. This ferry travels around Sydney Harbor in Australia. In San Francisco, the first U.S. hybrid ferry uses solar, wind, electric, and diesel power. Called the Hornblower Hybrid, it carries visitors to and from Alcatraz Island and Angel Island. (Alcatraz was once a federal prison, and Angel Island was once an immigration center. Each island is now a U.S. National Historic Landmark.) The Hornblower Hybrid also provides educational programs and facilities for meetings and large social events.

Ferry systems hire all kinds of workers. Each ferry employs a captain, deckhands, and engineers on board. On a ferryboat, you might help load cars (and passengers) on and off the ship. On land, ferry corporations need staff to take reservations and plan routes. Ferry systems also have IT, accounting, and legal services jobs, as well as environmental engineers, planners, and safety officers to keep everything ship-shape.

Because ferries are a form of mass transit, they help reduce the amount of fuel used by cars and other vehicles. People working for one of these systems can be sure that they are in a field that helps "green" our planet!

What We're Losin' by Cruisin'...

We've all seen TV commercials advertising voyages on bright, white, shiny cruise ships. They promise activities galore for kids and adults, and stops at beautiful destinations around the world.

But cruise ships also have a dark side. They still dump raw sewage into our oceans. Many of them generate tons of garbage. The smokestack on an average cruise ship blasts the emission-equivalent of 12,000 cars into the atmosphere every day. Yuck!

The problem is there are no international regulations when it comes to cruise ship pollution. Once they are three miles (4.8 km) offshore, these vessels are actually allowed to dump raw sewage in the ocean. The sewage is harmful to humans and to marine plants and animals.

DIRTY CRUISE SHIP STATS

Many cruise lines are taking steps to clean up their act at sea. While this is going on, recent statistics show that there is much work to be done. Here are some of the numbers:

Every day, the average cruise ship dumps into the water:

- 255,000 gallons (965,000 liters) of gray water (from showers, laundry, and dishes)

- 30,000 gallons (113,500 liters) of black water (sewage)

- 7,000 gallons (26,500 liters) of oil-contaminated water

A cruise ship releases three times more CO_2 (per passenger) than does a Boeing 747.

The average cruise ship churns out seven tons (six metric tons) of garbage a day. Most of it is burned and the ashes are dumped into the ocean. Many cruise ships simply dump the garbage directly into the water.

The waste shown here comes from a cruise ship sailing along the Nile River. It has been collected from the ship and transported to this river bank in Erdu, Egypt. Form here, it will be disposed of farther inland. An average cruise passenger generates four times more trash every day than a person at home on shore.

CAREER PROFILE

STEWARD OF THE SEA: CRUISE SHIP ENVIRONMENTAL OFFICER

I am the environmental officer on *Oasis of the Seas,* which is the biggest cruise ship in the world. My job has many duties. One is to make sure the ship complies with all regulations at sea and in port relating to environmental discharges to air and water. I also identify shipboard recycling opportunities and lead energy- and water-saving programs. I am also the onboard expert for chemical storage, use, and disposal. I train crew members in our "save the waves" program, and I respond to environmental inquiries from guests.

I have a bachelor's degree in Environmental Science and a master's degree in Pollution Control. Prior to working on ships, I had 10 years of experience in the military, private sector waste management, and local government. I did all of this work in the UK.

CONTINUED ON PAGE 35...

Peter Roy
Environmental Officer
Oasis of the Seas (home port: Port Everglades, Florida)
Royal Caribbean International

Food staff in a cruise ship's galley (kitchen). Cruises promise all the fun you can imagine—activities galore for kids and adults, more food than you could possibly sink your teeth into, and stops at beautiful destinations around the world. You can also imagine how much garbage a galley like this produces!

That's the bad news. The good news is that bad publicity about environmental crimes committed by cruise ships has led the industry to make some changes in recent years. While some cruise lines continue their bad habits, others are coming up with their own environmental initiatives, including the following:

- Onboard wastewater purification systems
- Disposing of garbage at landfills rather than at sea
- Water quality monitoring
- Low-flow toilets and showers
- Shipboard environmental officers
- More efficient, cleaner fuels
- Solar panels to generate onboard electricity

Living the High-Seas Life
Pretty much any job you can imagine doing on land, you can do on a cruise ship.

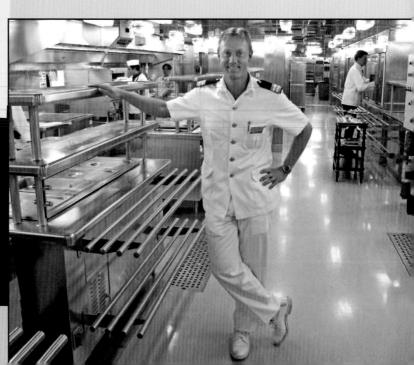

Cruise-ship jobs include administrative work, bartending, cleaning, entertaining, hairstyling, running computer systems, working in a fitness center or medical clinic, and cooking. There are also marine-related jobs such as being captain, first mate, or deckhand on a ship. Usually, you have to be at least 21 years old to work on a cruise ship. In fact, most staff members are in their 30s and 40s. Because cruise passengers tend to be an older crowd, cruise lines often prefer mature staff.

You must be prepared to share a small cabin with at least one other staff member and to be at sea for up to four months at a time.

The upside of working on a cruise ship is that you get to travel the world and meet all kinds of fascinating people. Plus, you get free food and accommodation!

There is another upside, this one for people who want to work for a cruise line and help the planet.

CAREER PROFILE

STEWARD OF THE SEA:
CRUISE SHIP
ENVIRONMENTAL OFFICER

...CONTINUED FROM PAGE 34

Typically, I work 10 weeks on the ship and 10 weeks off. I have an office onboard. In many ways, what I do is like an "office job," with meetings and report writing. Every day is different, however. You never stop learning, and you are working with colleagues who are the best at what they do.

What I love most about my work is the fact that the scenery is constantly changing. I also don't have to commute to work, and I get to meet interesting people. I move to a different ship every few years, so I never get bored.

This lifestyle would not suit everybody. You are away from home, friends, and family for extended periods. You need to be open to new ways of thinking and be able to solve problems quickly. Working on a massive cruise ship is no party. A lot happens behind the scenes, and so much of it requires hard work and sweat. People who think they can "cruise" along for the ride need not apply.

Peter Roy
Environmental Officer
Oasis of the Seas (home port: Port Everglades, Florida)
Royal Caribbean International

Environmental Officer Peter Roy monitors his ship's compliance with environmental regulations.

A GUIDING LIGHT TO THE SHIPPING BUSINESS

Green Marine is a U.S.-Canadian body that has come up with environmental guidelines for the shipping industry in North America. It started in 2008 with a focus on the St. Lawrence and Great Lakes corridor. Today, it covers all North American waters. What makes this organization special is that it was founded by people and associations already working in the marine industry. These folks wanted to help out Mother Nature by addressing a number of major shipping concerns. These include aquatic invasive species, air pollution, greenhouse gas emissions, and oily water. One major area of concern targeted by Green Marine: the unhealthy effects on ports caused by noise, odor, or light pollution from docked ships.

Organizations like Green Marine are always looking for new ideas, bright minds, and passionate young people to help address these issues.

With so many environmental initiatives afloat within the industry, there is more sensitivity to the needs of the environment aboard cruise ships. There are also bound to be more green jobs available. Some of these include helping cruise lines design, meet, and maintain higher levels of environmental responsibility. These practices will need people to plan and direct the use and disposal of fuel, wastewater, garbage, and other byproducts of life at sea.

Shipshape at Sea

Goods carried by freighters, tankers, and container ships account for 90 percent of the world's cargo transportation. Cargo ships are the least environmentally damaging mode of transport. Still, they have the same problems as cruise ships when it comes to soot, greenhouse gas emissions, and the risk of harming marine life. Most freighters and tankers carry crew members only, rarely transporting passengers. They therefore dump less garbage and sewage into the oceans. They are also subject to stricter pollution guidelines than are cruise ships.

Organizations like Green Marine are dedicated to making sure the shipping industry is kinder to our environment. These groups need designers, editors, writers, and technicians to produce Web sites and newsletters. Here, a designer is shown working at her electronic "sketchpad."

One increased risk with certain vessels—oil tankers, to be exact—is the risk of an oil spill. Such a spill can be catastrophic for ecosystems and wildlife in the water and onshore. Because of new regulations and better ship design, the number of major oil spills from ships has dropped in the past 30 years from 25 a year to four a year. That rate continues to decline. Thank goodness!

Like cruise ships, transport ships have had to clean up their air emissions in recent years. Plus, they will be subject to even stricter rules to be phased in starting in 2012. The easiest thing ships can do to reduce emissions and save fuel is to simply slow down. If every ship in the global fleet slowed down by 10 percent, emissions would drop by 23 percent. Some shipping companies have realized this and are already cutting their speeds.

To help the shipping industry kick the high-fuel habit, some ports have installed onshore power systems. Now some vessels can plug in to get electricity while docked. This allows them to avoid running their diesel engines all the time. New hull designs and adjustments to propellers, coatings, and mechanics are helping ships cut through the water more efficiently.

> "Ships traveling at slow speeds ... [are] roughly 10 times more efficient than trucks, and at least 100 times more efficient than air transport."
>
> Ellycia Harrould-Kolieb, *Shipping Impacts on Climate: A Source with Solutions* (Washington, D.C.: Oceana, 2008)

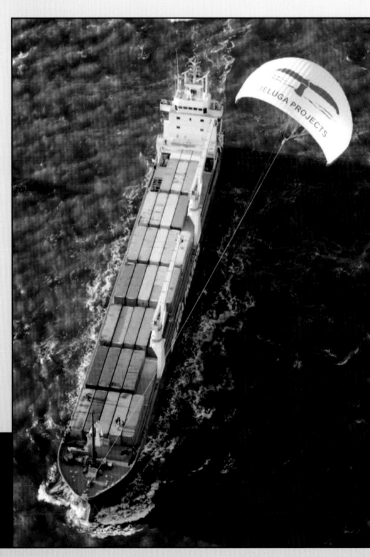

The SkySail, shown here flying above a cargo ship, is a parachute that attaches to the bow of the ship. It helps save fuel and reduce emissions by capturing the wind and pulling the vessel along.

SUN AND SEA: SOLAR YACHT DESIGNER

At 16, I had the good fortune to attend a talk from one of the world's top yacht designers, Andrew Winch. He opened my eyes to the world of yacht design. I had sailed from a very young age. So, with my love of art, plus my design flair, my ideal career was born! I attended a four-year course in Transport Design at Coventry University in England.

As a yacht designer, I create new and exciting designs. These are specifically geared for the owners' use and their day-to-day enjoyment on the water. I sketch and draw (by hand) various designs that include the yachts' look, styling, size, and color.

My recent award-winning project, "Soliloquy," is the first zero-emission superyacht concept. The yacht I designed is carbon-neutral. It also runs from harnessing the power of nature. It captures solar energy and is propelled by the wind using a new type of sail—rigid sails. When it is sunny or windy, there is no need for fossil fuels.

For those who are passionate about the sea, boats, and design, there is no better or more rewarding job on Earth. You take an idea that you sketched out on paper. Then you develop it into three dimensions on a computer. You then see it as a "sculptured form" in real life.

My profession is my passion. I will continue to enjoy creating revolutionary yacht designs for many years to come.

Alastair Callender
Creative Design Director
Callender Designs
Chichester, West Sussex, UK

Zero-emission superyacht designer
Alastair Callender

A Career You Create

Sometimes, the best jobs in the world are the ones you design yourself. If you are passionate about boating and protecting the environment, you might come up with your own special project to work on. Some inventors have already done just that and have designed some amazing new watercraft. Here are a few:

E/S Orcelle. Named after a type of dolphin, the *E/S Orcelle* is powered by sunlight, wind, and waves. These three energy sources are all plentiful at sea. "E/S" stands for *Environmentally sound Ship*. Rigid dorsal-fin sails harness the wind. The sails also house solar panels to capture the Sun's energy. Meanwhile, 12 underwater fins draw energy from the waves. That energy, in turn, is converted to hydrogen, electrical, or mechanical energy. Hailed as the world's first truly environmentally friendly cargo ship, *Orcelle* has been on the drawing board since 2004. The Scandinavian shipping company that designed it, Wallenius Wilhelmsen, expects this ship to be sailing by 2025.

Plastiki. In 2010, the *Plastiki,* a boat made from 12,500 plastic bottles, made a four-month voyage from San Francisco, California, to Sydney, Australia. The 60-foot (18.3 m) ship and its crew were all about reusing, reducing, recycling, and raising awareness. In addition to the plastic bottles, the boat featured a mast and sail made of recycled materials. Its construction also included organic glue made from cashew nuts and sugar cane. Onboard power was generated by solar panels, wind turbines, and bicycle generators. These generators, which run with pedal power, also helped the crew keep fit. Crew members showered with rainwater and grew their own fruit and vegetables on board.

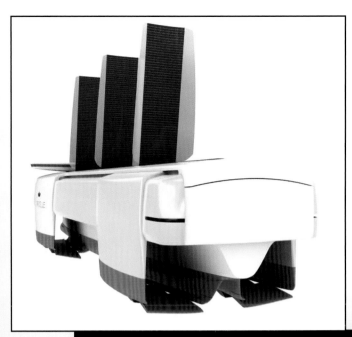

As this illustration shows, the *E/S Orcelle* has finlike sails that harness wind and solar power. Beneath the environmentally friendly cargo ship, more fins capture energy from waves.

This shot of *Plastiki* shows off two of the craft's many environmentally friendly features—solar panels used to draw energy from the Sun (far right) and recycled plastic bottles used as building materials (along the side).

The catamaran *sun21* motors across New York Harbor toward Manhattan as it completes its historic solar-powered, 7,000-mile (11,200 km) transatlantic voyage.

sun21. This catamaran made history in May 2007. That was when it became the first solar-powered boat to cross the Atlantic Ocean without using a drop of oil. Designed by Swiss ship builder Mark Wüst, *sun21* made the 7,000-mile (11,200 km) trip in five months.

Suntory Mermaid II. Japanese eco-sailor Kenichi Horie had already sailed solo across the Pacific Ocean in a pedal-powered boat and two different solar-powered boats. In 2008, he made a trip from Hawaii to Japan in the world's first wave-powered boat, the *Suntory Mermaid II.* Two front-end "fins" move up and down, like a dolphin's tail, to propel the vessel through the water. It took Kenichi 110 days to make the trip. The boat, made from recycled aluminum, uses solar energy to power its electrical systems.

Tûranor PlanetSolar. In September 2010, the *Tûranor PlanetSolar*, the world's largest solar-powered boat, left Monaco on a six-month around-the-world cruise. Its objective was to prove that solar power could be the way of the future for watercraft.

The brainchild of a pair of Swiss and German designers, the vessel's upper deck is covered with 5,800 square feet (539 sq m) of solar panels. It also has batteries that can store three days' worth of power.

It took a team effort to make *PlanetSolar* a reality. The boat was produced by people with a variety of skills. These included invention and design, marketing the boat's features and "look," physically building the craft, and putting the boat through its paces on the high seas.

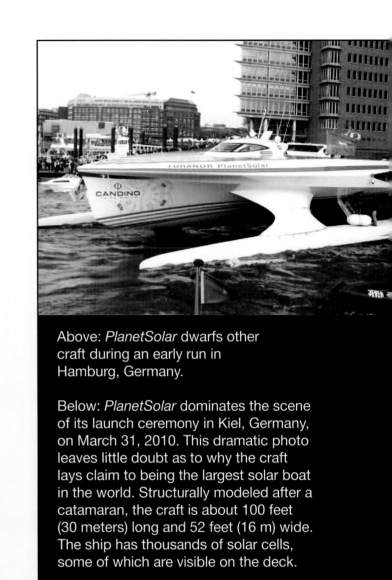

Above: *PlanetSolar* dwarfs other craft during an early run in Hamburg, Germany.

Below: *PlanetSolar* dominates the scene of its launch ceremony in Kiel, Germany, on March 31, 2010. This dramatic photo leaves little doubt as to why the craft lays claim to being the largest solar boat in the world. Structurally modeled after a catamaran, the craft is about 100 feet (30 meters) long and 52 feet (16 m) wide. The ship has thousands of solar cells, some of which are visible on the deck.

CHAPTER 4

UP, UP, AND AWAY— AIR TRAVEL

Becoming a member of the ground crew at an airport is one way of working to assure the safety and comfort of passengers.

Many of us, at some point in our lives, have tried flapping our arms or jumping off a picnic table with an open umbrella, hoping we could fly. Unlike the birds or the fictional Mary Poppins, though, the only way most humans can become airborne is to ride in a plane or a helicopter.

Flight Crew or Ground Crew

Do you love the idea of soaring through the skies? If so, maybe you'd like to have a career as an airline pilot or flight engineer, a flight attendant or flight instructor, a helicopter pilot, or even a sky marshal.

On the other hand, you may be someone who has a passion for flight but likes the idea of working on the ground. If so, it's good to know that not all careers related to air travel happen in the sky. Think about the fellows who actually created air travel in the first place—the Wright brothers.

An airline flight attendant demonstrates the safety features on her plane. If travel and being responsible for the safety and comfort of passengers in the air appeal to you, then working as a flight attendant might be your ideal job.

In 1903, Wilbur and Orville Wright designed the first airplane—the first that actually flew, that is. They worked at their drawing board and tinkered in their workshop. During most of their work, they had their feet firmly on the ground.

Even though the airplane has already been invented, it doesn't mean there is nothing left to try when it comes to flying the skies. New fuels and fuel sources need to be researched and developed. New airplane designs need to be created. New air traffic systems and even new types of aircraft are all waiting to be discovered or developed. The industry needs people like you to design or invent them!

GREENER SKIES AHEAD

We know that airplanes produce greenhouse gases. We also know it's not realistic to stop all air travel, so what can we do to lessen the impact of the flights we take? Many airlines have set up programs, called carbon offsets, that allow you to contribute to projects around the world that actually help the environment. That way, the CO_2 produced during your flight is counterbalanced by energy-efficient projects elsewhere.

In Canada, for example, Air Canada passengers can contribute to a reforestation (tree-planting) project in British Columbia, a tire recycling program in Quebec, or a landfill gas recovery project in Ontario. In the United States, Continental Airlines offers passengers the offset options of reforestation and renewable energy programs.

Airlines work with groups that run carbon offset projects. Maybe you'd like to research and design such a project, or work with an airline to evaluate and choose the best projects to offer its passengers. Or maybe you'd like to be the marketing person who lets passengers know what the airline is doing to be more environmentally conscious.

Might using airships for travel or transportation be making a comeback? They are quiet, easy to maneuver, and environmentally friendly. The craft shown here is electrically powered, seats several passengers and crew members in its cabin, and flies safely, even at low altitudes.

FUELING FUTURE FLIGHT

Jet fuel, or kerosene, is different than car fuel. It has different performance and safety properties. This means that the alternative fuel sources being developed for automobiles won't work for planes.

Any fuel designed to replace jet fuel must be sustainable, effective, and cost efficient. It must also be a "drop-in" fuel. This means that aircraft engines don't have to be modified to use it. Commercial airliners are designed to fly for about 30 years. The engine is the most expensive part. Replacing it to adapt a plane to a different fuel partway through its lifespan is just too expensive.

The aircraft industry is always on the lookout for scientists, researchers, and test pilots to help develop and test new fuels in the lab and in the air.

Ups and Downs of Flying Machines

We may travel for business or pleasure, for sightseeing or for military maneuvers. We may be traveling short or long distances. Whatever the need, we have a number of choices when it comes to taking to the skies.

We can travel in airplanes, large and small, in helicopters, seaplanes, and private jets. For the more adventuresome, there are even hot air balloons and gliders!

For those of us who love to travel to faraway places, airplanes are the fastest, most economical way to get us where we're going. When we want to fly, most of us think of using the commercial airline industry. In 2009, the world's airlines transported about 2.2 billion passengers and 40 million tons (36 million metric tons) of freight around the globe. About 40 percent of international tourists travel by air, and the industry employs 32 million people worldwide.

In June 2010, at an air show in Germany, the Diamond DA42 NG, a small, four-seat, twin-engine plane, made the first-ever flight fully powered by algae-based biofuel. This plane may have been the first to fly solely on algae-based fuel. It wasn't the first to try biofuel of any sort, however. Previous test flights with biofuel-kerosene blends have proven that these new fuels are feasible options, worthy of further exploration.

Most planes fly with more than three-quarters of the seats filled (compared to half the seats in trains). This means that a lot of people travel on one tank of fuel. In addition, aircraft are becoming more and more fuel efficient every year. Today's aircraft fly three times farther on the same amount of fuel as did the planes of 40 years ago. Right now, air travel accounts for just 2 percent of human-made carbon dioxide (CO_2) emissions.

Despite these positive statistics overall, there are exceptions in individual uses of aircraft. For each mile (1.6 km) traveled, a large airplane uses more fuel than 300 regular cars. It also spews huge amounts of greenhouse gases into the atmosphere. Because air travel is growing every year, CO_2 emissions are also expected to grow to 3 percent of total human-made emissions by 2050. The industry is working hard to increase fuel efficiency. The growth in air travel could cancel out any fuel savings, however, unless researchers can come up with a new fuel source. Maybe that's where you come in!

LITTLE GREEN FUEL CELLS

In recent years, the aircraft industry has made it a top priority to find its own fuel alternatives. Researchers believe they have found the answer in biofuels—specifically, algae-based biofuels. To date, the most promising feedstock for aircraft fuel is algae. These microscopic, plantlike organisms can be grown in deserts, polluted water, salt water, and other places where plants and other life-forms normally can't survive. Algae thrive on carbon dioxide (CO_2). They can thus absorb any CO_2 released during the pressing and refining process, making the whole cycle carbon-neutral. Algae grow so quickly they can produce 15 times more oil per square mile (or sq km) as other biofuel crops. Also, they don't need excessive amounts of pesticides or fertilizers. All of these factors make algae an efficient, economical, and environmentally friendly feedstock for making biofuel.

These researchers are cultivating microscopic algae in the lab. The algae are being grown as part of the Shamash project. The goal of this project is to produce biofuel from algae and other microscopic organisms that can thrive on compounds such as carbon dioxide.

Getting Powered the Natural Way

Today, jet fuel is the energy source of choice for most aircraft. It is also one of the dirtiest fuels around. Fortunately for our atmosphere, researchers are hard at work creating cleaner, more efficient energy alternatives. Developing these fuels is also a source of jobs for people who want to work in air travel and help the environment at the same time.

Some of the careers in developing biofuels provide work for chemists, biochemists, microbiologists, agriculture specialists, engineers, lab managers, and lab technicians. As the industry progresses, people will also be needed to farm and manage the raw materials, or feedstocks, for biofuels.

Of course, biofuels aren't the only energy sources taking off when it comes to powering aircraft. Solar power and electricity are two fossil fuel-free and emission-free alternatives on the horizon.

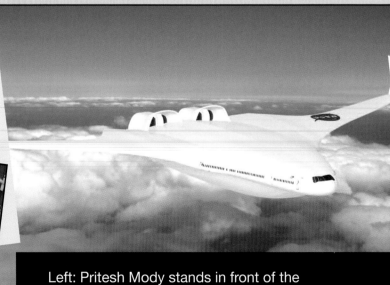

Left: Pritesh Mody stands in front of the Space Shuttle *Enterprise* at the National Air and Space Museum in Washington, D.C. Above: A plane bears the NASA logo that Pritesh helped design at MIT.

In 1990, a little plane called *Sunseeker I* crossed the United States. This solar-electric hybrid made history by completing the longest journey ever made by a solar-powered aircraft. In the summer of 2009, the *Sunseeker II* spent three months touring Europe. This refined, more efficient, more powerful plane became the first solar-powered aircraft to fly over the Alps. The two-seat *Sunseeker III* is now in development.

All three of these planes use battery power to take off and climb. Once airborne, they simply soak up the sun to keep aloft and soaring.

Imagine being the inventor and pilot of the *Sunseeker* series of planes! That's Eric Raymond's job. After studying aeronautical engineering, Eric helped build unmanned aircraft for the U.S. military. He also served as test pilot for a human-powered (pedal-powered) aircraft. That inspired him to design and build the first *Sunseeker*.

For many years, the *Sunseekers* were the only solar-powered airplanes that flew with a pilot aboard. Prior to these craft, solar-powered planes were remote-controlled. Today, another solar-powered craft, the *Solar Impulse*, has taken to the skies.

"Basically, the *Sunseeker* is an ultralight sailplane, with a top speed of only 70 knots (80 mph or 130 km/h). Birds are not frightened away and often fly in formation with me for long periods."

Eric Raymond
Inventor and pilot,
Sunseeker planes

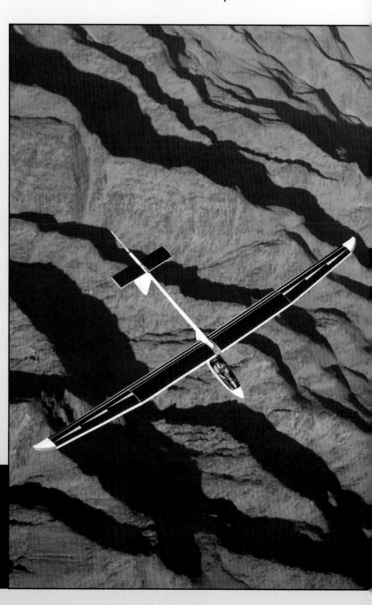

Sunseeker II is shown prior to its historic flight over the Alps in 2009. The plane flies so slowly and smoothly that the pilot's canopy is often kept open during good weather.

THE SKY'S THE LIMIT:
TEST PILOT AND CEO OF
AN ALTERNATIVE-ENERGY
AIRCRAFT MANUFACTURER

Together with Bertrand Piccard, I share the leadership of *Solar Impulse*. My main role has been to set up a skilled team of engineers, electricians, and specialists. All of these people worked together to imagine, design, build, test, and fly an airplane that had never been built before.

I am also a pilot, and I made the first night flight of *Solar Impulse*. In that sense, my role is also to show that the aircraft we create is functional.

My daily life is to work closely with the team and find the best solutions. I don't have a proper office. I work in many different places with the team, partners, and suppliers.

To do this type of work, you have to be curious and like challenges, especially when people say things are impossible.

As a passionate pilot, my most special days are the flight-testing days. Flying through the night, after seven years of work, was just amazing!

Developing technologies that allow energy savings is essential today! We don't have the choice anymore. The price of oil will climb, and we won't be able to continue to fly as we do today. We have to seek new solutions quickly.

André Borschberg
Chief Executive Officer
Solar Impulse SA
Nyon, Switzerland

In June 2010, this plane flew a record 26 hours non-stop. It became the first-ever aircraft to fly day and night without fuel and, therefore, without pollution.

The test pilot for the night flight was André Borschberg. A former Swiss Air Force pilot, he is now CEO and co-founder of Solar Impulse SA, the group behind the *Solar Impulse* project. "I've been a pilot for 40 years now, but this flight has been the most incredible one of my flying career," says André. "Just sitting there and watching the battery charge level rise and rise thanks to the sun.... And then that suspense, not knowing whether we were going to manage to stay up in the air the whole night." He did!

Solar Impulse test pilot and team leader André Borschberg gives a thumbs-up from the cockpit of his craft.

The ultimate goal of the *Solar Impulse* project is to fly around the world in a solar-powered aircraft beginning in 2013. Of course, a project like that requires a huge team of people. More than 50 specialists from six countries design, refine, build, and maintain the prototype aircraft. In addition, about 100 other people serve as advisers.

In addition to pilots, *Solar Impulse* team members include structural, design, electrical, mechanical, and software engineers. Technical support includes assembly technicians and mechanics. Rounding out the team are traffic controllers, meteorologists, and marketing and administrative support. As research and development of alternative-powered aircraft continues to soar in the coming years, so will career opportunities for people who want to build, operate, and maintain such aircraft. Is that something you might do?

Solar Impulse at sunset. In this dramatic shot, the solar-powered craft seems to be catching the last rays of the Sun as it prepares to fly off into the night sky.

"The history of aviation is marked by people achieving extraordinary things, despite the conventional wisdom of the time telling them it couldn't be done."

Beginner's Guide to Aviation Biofuels
(Geneva, Switzerland: Air Transport Action Group, 2009)

These parts of scrapped aircraft, while of no value as they now exist, can be worth tens of thousands of dollars if recycled for their metal or used to provide parts for other planes.

Reduce, Reuse, Recycle… a Jumbo Jet!?

Perhaps working on the research, science, and invention side of air transportation isn't your thing. If you'd rather work in a mechanical field or operate heavy equipment, then tearing apart airplanes for a living might be fun!

Every year, about 450 commercial aircraft are completely scrapped. In the next 15 to 20 years, 6,000 more aircraft are scheduled to be trashed. That's what happens to a plane that has reached the end of its lifespan or aircraft whose owners can no longer afford to operate them. Thanks to aircraft recycling companies around the world, most of the airplane's materials and parts stay out of landfills.

"There are a lot of materials that are very valuable in aircraft," says Jim Toomey, president of Evergreen Air Center in Arizona, one of the busiest aircraft recyclers in North America. "If you're just taking apart a plane, you could be throwing away $40,000 to $50,000 worth of stuff."

That "stuff" includes everything from the engine (which is either stripped down and sold for parts or repaired, if possible), to flight deck instruments. It also includes air conditioning, wing flaps, wheels, doors, and windows. After the fuselage, or body of the aircraft, has been gutted, an excavator starts chomping away at the metal. The fuselage is then torn into small pieces, melted down, and reused in new products.

Who buys recycled bits of airplanes? Well, airlines buy parts for training purposes. This includes teaching everything from emergency procedures and baggage handling to how to open an airplane door. Airline manufacturers buy certified parts for reuse in new aircraft. TV and film production companies also buy all kinds of bits and pieces. These companies use the parts to create sets for shows that feature airplanes. For example, the jet that crashed in the first episode of the long-running TV show *Lost* was a recycled airliner.

FLYING INTO THE FUTURE

It sounds like something out of *Star Wars*, but believe it or not, one idea flying around these days is the concept of an airplane that would fly just outside Earth's atmosphere. It would be propelled by liquid hydrogen. The only byproduct would be water vapor.

The term *aerospace* refers to the science of both airplanes and spacecraft. Such a plane would create new opportunities for people working in the aerospace industry. For starters, designing and building a craft that takes off and lands as an airplane and yet is capable of traveling at great speeds and withstanding the rigors of outer space would provide plenty of challenges to engineers. Beyond that would lie new opportunities for crew members, ground crew and other service and mechanical workers, and airport and security personnel.

CHAPTER 5

A NEW WAY—
URBAN PLANNING

Making cities greener, more pedestrian friendly, and attractive to new residents is one goal of smart urban planning.

The development of the suburbs posed one of the biggest challenges in terms of transportation.

In the 1950s and 1960s, having a house in suburbia, with a front yard and backyard, a driveway, and a carport or garage, was the dream of most families. People who could afford it moved out of the town centers to the edges of the urbanized areas. Subdivisions started taking over farmland and forest, and people who lived in the suburbs drove their cars into the city to work every day.

Making Our Towns Green

All those cars traveling between the suburbs and the city every day are pouring huge amounts of pollutants into the atmosphere. For the sake of cleaning up the air alone, it's time to find ways to make cities and neighborhoods more "green." Strangely, re-inventing communities to make them more green means going back to some of

Architects and city planners meet over drawings and models. A career in urban planning can lead to creating more sustainable city environments.

the ways of the past. These include people living closer together, in neighborhoods where they can also work, with stores and businesses within walking distance of homes. It may also mean commuters traveling by train, or other forms of public transit, into the city center.

People who plan such communities to make them more sustainable are called urban planners or city planners. Many others are also involved in the process of creating sustainable cities and neighborhoods. These include traffic engineers, landscape designers, environmentalists, architects, artists, and politicians, to name a few. Maybe the future of community design is in *your* future!

Healthy and Happy

If you were asked to design a new community, what elements would you think are important in a healthy neighborhood or town?

New Urbanism is the name of a design concept to create healthy, sustainable communities. Such communities are quiet, attractive places where people

CAREER PROFILE

ON THE GREEN ROAD: STREET DESIGN ENGINEER

I work in the Civil Design Section of the Portland (Oregon) Bureau of Transportation as a street design engineer and a green street coordinator. My job is to develop green street designs.

I spend the bulk of my time attending technical meetings and work sessions, discussing projects, and developing design guidelines and policies. I also work with people in many other disciplines, including traffic engineering, structural engineering, signals and street lighting, and environmental engineering. Mostly I work in an office, but I often go out in the field for site visits, too.

I feel the greatest accomplishment so far in my career is my contribution to the City of Portland's green street details and the implementation of green infrastructure. A "green street" encompasses elements such as drainage ditches called bio-swales for storm water treatment and disposal. It also involves reusing and recycling materials, promoting non-motorized transportation, such as walking and biking, and using more sustainable materials and resources. We are really figuring this out as we go along, and it is exciting!

Nicole Blanchard
Engineer
City of Portland
Bureau of
Transportation

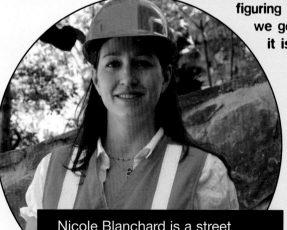

Nicole Blanchard is a street design engineer and green street coordinator in Portland, Oregon.

RESEARCHING AND DEVELOPING A GREENER CEMENT

Cars and trucks aren't the only threat to the environment when it comes to our road systems. The roads themselves are part of the problem. Cement production is responsible for about 5 percent of global CO_2 emissions—and cement is the main ingredient in road concrete.

With that in mind, a group of researchers from England, Scotland, and India is exploring a new way to make cement. Using waste materials such as ash and rice husks instead of limestone and clay, this process reduces the carbon footprint of cement production. A *carbon footprint* is the amount of CO_2 emitted due to the consumption of fossil fuels by a particular person or group.

Meanwhile, researchers in the United States are working on other eco-friendly cements. One of these actually removes CO_2 from the environment as it is processed.

can live and work. In these places, networks of parks and landscaped walkways create spaces where people feel safe and have access to all the shops, services, and recreation facilities they might need—without driving. That is one of the keys to New Urbanism—no cars, or at least car-free zones. The idea is to build pedestrian-friendly, or *walkable*, compact communities, with user-friendly public transit systems.

People who live in a pedestrian-friendly town or neighborhood are not dependent on their cars, so they save money and are healthier because they walk or cycle. They also do not add to the traffic jams and air pollution that come with driving everywhere.

Doing It Right

Many European cities are first-rate when it comes to sustainable urban design. That's partly because they tend to be older, more historic cities than those in North America. Many European cities were designed centuries ago, before cars were invented, so they were built with car-free qualities in mind.

One of the world's most sustainable cities is Copenhagen, Denmark. Copenhagen started with a sensible structure—a grid of narrow, medieval streets. Modern city planners didn't stop there. For the past 50 years, they have worked to maintain and improve the city's pedestrian-friendly quality of life. It all started in 1962, when the city turned its main street into a pedestrian-only walkway. Since then, planners have added more pedestrian streets. Planners are gradually reducing the number of parking spaces, turning former parking lots into public squares and parks, and encouraging residents to move into the city center. Today, more than 6,000 people live in the heart of Copenhagen, and most of them don't own cars.

The city encourages bicycle commuting by continually creating and expanding bicycle lanes. Today, about 34 percent of residents cycle to work.

In the United States, Portland, Oregon, comes out on top as the most sustainable city. Its ranking is based on such factors as public transit use, walkability, bikability, clean air and water, city planning and land use, energy and climate policies, and renewable energy use. In the 1970s, other U.S. cities were embracing their cars and building up suburbia. At the same time, city planners in Portland started thinking green. Back then, they introduced strict land-use policies to limit the growth of the city

Above: Venice, Italy, is considered one of the greatest pedestrian cities in the world. Instead of roadways, it has a network of pathways, canals, and bridges. Venice is designed for people to get around on foot or by boat.

Below: For decades, Copenhagen, Denmark, has been a model for New Urban planners. Its historic buildings have been preserved, and its main street has been turned into a pedestrian-friendly walkway. In the summer, its city center is alive with outdoor cafés, public squares, and street performers.

BIKES IN THE CITY

In 2008, the SmartBike system in Washington, D.C., became the first major bicycle-sharing program in the United States. By then, bike-sharing programs had been successfully operated in Asia and Europe for more than a decade. The first large-scale, urban bike-share program started in Copenhagen, Denmark, in 1995. The most successful program, called Vélib', is in Paris, France. It features more than 20,000 bicycles available at more than 1,600 stations throughout the city. Even smaller cities can accommodate bike sharing. For example, Caen, which is northwest of Paris, has 250 bikes and 40 stations.

The idea is simple. Using a credit card or a subscription card, you rent a bicycle at one station in the city. After you have ridden the bike, you turn it in at the same station or at any other station in the network. The goal is to reduce the number of cars in city centers by providing affordable bicycle rentals.

and increase density. Even today, the city's goal is to be what they call a "20-minute city." This means that Portlanders will never spend more than 20 minutes in their cars to go to work, school, shops, or recreation activities.

Old Town, New Tricks

If you are an urban planner working within a city that is already built for cars, how do you help that city and its residents kick the driving habit? Well, you'd use some Smart Growth techniques.

V'eol, in Caen, France, is one of many bike-sharing systems in European cities.

Smart Growth means this: If a city or town is growing, planners design the growth so it happens in compact, pedestrian-friendly neighborhoods within the existing city limits. This revitalizes existing urban areas instead of taking over more farmland or forest to add more car-friendly suburbs. Smart Growth communities are walkable and sustainable. Cycle paths and sidewalks lead to small village centers, featuring shops, services, and recreation facilities. All that walking means fewer cars on the roads.

FROM MEAN STREETS TO GREEN STREETS

For neighborhoods that are already fully developed, here are some things planners propose to help green the streets:

- **Traffic calming measures, such as traffic circles, zigzagging barriers, and speed bumps, force cars to slow down. This saves fuel and helps make the streets safer.**

- **Many large cities are adding bike lanes to the roadways to encourage cycling.**

- **Traffic engineers are able to time streetlights so that if a car is traveling at the speed limit, it won't have to stop for red lights. That cuts down on speeding for short stretches that wastes fuel, and reduces the number of cars wasting gas idling at stoplights.**

- **Many municipalities are changing zoning to allow live/work options. Such options permit people to run their businesses out of their homes, so they don't have to drive to work.**

Portland, Oregon, ranks at the top of most lists of sustainable U.S. cities. Clockwise from upper left shows a street market, a spiral pedestrian walkway, and a stop along the city's light rail transit system.

In 2000, a U.S.-wide organization called Smart Growth America was founded. Its goal is to promote sustainable urban growth. It also pushes for the protection of farmland and the creation of healthier cities, affordable housing, and green transportation. The Smart Growth Canada Network started in 2003 with similar objectives.

Green Transportation for Tomorrow

Since the early 20th century, we've spent so much time coming and going that we haven't stopped to realize what all this transportation—and reliance on fossil fuels—is doing to our planet. The good news is that it's not too late for Planet Earth.

So, are you someone who cares about the environment? Do you love to be on the go? Do you love helping others on their journeys through life or enjoy finding solutions to pollution problems? If your answer to any of these questions is "yes," then perhaps a career in green transportation will take you places in your future. The possibilities seem endless!

The bicycle is still the greenest way to travel on wheels. From designing bicycles and bicycle-friendly environments to selling and servicing bikes in a shop, the bicycle is also a great way to go if you're looking for a job or a career in green transportation.

START YOUR GREEN FUTURE NOW...

It's exciting to have plans and dreams for the future. It's also exciting to try new things. Here are some fun projects to help you find out what you enjoy doing and to whet your appetite for your future career.

BOATING FOR FUN—AND HEALTHY WATER

If you sail, kayak, canoe, pedal, or row your boat, congratulations: You're already living green! But if your family has a motorboat, here are some tips to help you get started as an eco-friendly boater:

- Keep the motor maintained to make sure it operates as efficiently as possible. About 30 percent of fuel and oil used in boating ends up in the water.
- Dispose of all oil, batteries, antifreeze, cleaning products, paints, and their containers at a certified recycling center.
- Fill the gas tank slowly to avoid spills, fill it on shore, and don't overfill it.
- Always have oil- and gas-absorbing rags on board in case of a spill.
- Take the shortest route from Point A to Point B to use as little fuel as possible.
- Study marine charts to make sure you steer clear of sensitive ecosystems.
- Use eco-friendly cleaning products on your boat.
- Recycle fishing line. Don't throw it overboard where it may entangle a fish or bird. Never throw garbage overboard.
- Seek out green marinas.

BE SMART, BE SAFE!

Please get permission from the adult who cares for you before making trips to new places or volunteering in your free time. Always let him or her know where you are going and who you are meeting. If you are getting paid for any kind of work, check the laws where you live to make sure you are old enough to have a part-time job.

CHARGE UP YOUR AUTOMOTIVE KNOWLEDGE

Learn more about electric vehicles (EVs)! Why not get together with a group of friends and rent the movie *Who Killed the Electric Car?* Then, with the help of an adult, arrange a visit to a dealership that sells cars made by a manufacturer who believes in EVs. There are many that are making EVs top priority right now. At the dealership, ask questions about electric cars. Ask to sit in an EV, if the showroom has one. You can even do some comparison shopping at the dealer or online. Then decide which EV you would get if you could buy one!

SPECIAL DELIVERY

If you have a bicycle, offer to deliver letters to the nearest mailbox or return books to the local library for your neighbors and friends. It'll be a little like being a bicycle courier in a big city!

OFFER TIPS ON GREENER DRIVING

Now that you've learned about green transportation, maybe you could teach the adult drivers in your life a thing or two about driving cleaner and greener. For example, you might help your parents plan their errands for a day. You could make sure they take the most efficient route instead of taking a bunch of short trips or backtracking. Take a look in the trunk of the car. Is there anything in there your family doesn't need to be carrying around? Less weight in the car means using less gas. Learn how to check the air pressure in the car tires. Then check them regularly, or ask an adult to check them, to make sure they are at the correct pressure. If the pressure is lower than recommended, the surface of the tire against the road will be greater. This increases the tire's friction and "drag" with the road, requiring more gas to keep the car moving at its usual speeds.

GREENING YOUR NEIGHBORHOOD

Imagine you are an urban planner or urban designer. Take a walk around your neighborhood and see what sorts of things could be done to encourage people to walk more and drive less.

GLOSSARY

biofuel A renewable fuel made from algae, plant sources such as corn, or even used vegetable oil

bio-isoprene Synthetic (artificial) rubber made from plant materials

bio-swale A long drainage ditch, or swale, filled with vegetation, compost, or small stones to filter out pollution as surface water flows through, often as runoff during rainstorms

biotechnology A field of science that uses processes found in the natural world to create new products or to modify existing products; examples: a naturally produced mold that is purified to form penicillin and the natural fermentation of fruit that is used to make wine

black carbon Soot

black water Wastewater that contains raw sewage

bow The front end of a boat

byproduct A product that results from the production or manufacture of something else; example: refining sugar cane to produce sugar, with molasses as a byproduct

carbon-neutral Referring to a process that uses as much carbon as it produces. For example, if carbon dioxide is released into the air when coal is converted to electricity, trees can be planted nearby to use up that carbon dioxide.

Compressed Natural Gas (CNG) Natural gas that has been super-compressed, making it super-concentrated, so it takes up less space

emission A substance discharged into the air

EV (electric vehicle) charging stations Like gas stations, where cars fill up, but in this case, the cars are recharged with electricity

feedstock A natural, raw material that is used to make a product. For example, corn is a feedstock used to make ethanol.

fermentation A naturally occurring food process that converts carbohydrates to alcohol

fossil fuel A fuel source that started as a microorganism buried deep beneath Earth's surface and eventually converted to oil, coal, or gas

fuselage The main body of an airplane; the part where passengers sit

gray water Wastewater from activities such as laundry, showering, bathing, and dishwashing

greenhouse gases Gases that are released into Earth's atmosphere when fossil fuels are burned. Carbon dioxide, or CO_2, is the main greenhouse gas. These gases have always been present in our environment but are now at record and potentially harmful levels.

hybrid Any vehicle that combines two or more types of power. The gasoline-electric car is the most common hybrid today.

hydrogen fuel cell A device in which hydrogen and oxygen are mixed in a chemical reaction that produces electricity

industrialized nations Countries that have a high level of economic development

invasive species Species, or varieties, of plants or animals that live in a location where they didn't originate; usually refers to a species that is harmful to native species and ecosystems

New Urbanism A design concept to create healthy, sustainable communities where people can live and work, with shops, services, parks, and recreation facilities within walking distance

organism A living thing. Plants, animals, fungi, algae, and bacteria are all organisms.

sky marshal An undercover law officer who travels on airplanes to protect passengers in case of an attempted hijacking

Smart Growth A way of planning and development in a town or city so that growth happens within existing city limits and doesn't use up any more land. Smart Growth communities are compact and pedestrian friendly, with shops, services, and recreation facilities within walking distance.

subdivisions Large areas of land that are divided up into smaller housing lots

suburbia A residential area within driving distance of the city center, where the population is more spread out than in urban areas

sustainable Able to go on into the future. Sustainable resources, such as plants and algae, can be used with little or no long-term effect on the environment.

synthetic Something made by a chemical process but designed to look like the real thing. For example, many women's purses are made of synthetic leather, which looks real but isn't.

unrefined Not processed, impure. Unrefined oil is oil as it comes out of the ground, before it is processed for use as fuel.

walkable Pedestrian friendly, referring to places where walking is encouraged

*www.youtube.com/watch?v=G1L4GUA8ar
    Y&feature=channel*
This is a fun, animated video that shows
how air traffic around the world changes
throughout the day.

www.aircanada.com/en/about/career/
If you're interested in having a career in
the air, this Web site describes all kinds
of aviation-related careers, including
becoming a pilot or flight attendant.
The site also includes descriptions of
customer service, maintenance, and
ground crew work. It also lists some of
the skills and education required to do
these kinds of jobs, introduces you to
people who do some of these jobs, and
describes a typical day-in-the-life of
some airline employees.

*www.sonyclassics.com/whokilledthe
    electriccar/electric.html?detectflash=
    false&*
This is a really cool, interactive Web site
where you can learn all about the history
of the electric car. Also on board: the pros
and cons of all kinds of cars, including
hybrid and gas-fueled vehicles and those
run by hydrogen fuel cells and biodiesel.
It also gives you some ideas about how
you can make a difference today.

www.careerontrack.ca/
www.bls.gov/oco/ocos244.htm
Thinking of a career on the rails? Here are
two Web sites with everything you need to
know about working in the train industry in
Canada and in the United States.

www.howstuffworks.com/maglev-train.htm
This site is all about Maglev (or magnetic
levitation) trains, one of the fastest,
quietest, most environmentally friendly
modes of transportation going. Check
out the video of the train in action!

*www.cityryde.com/blog/
    a-documentary-on-bike-sharing/*
If you have eight minutes to spare,
take a look at this excerpt from a larger
documentary about bicycling. This
segment is all about Amsterdam's cycling
culture and bike-sharing program.

www.cnu.org/Intro_to_new_urbanism
www.newurbanism.org
These excellent Web sites address
sustainable urban design, green
transportation, and global warming, with
a lot of links to other Web sites, books,
videos, articles, and other resources.

ABOUT THE AUTHOR

Diane Dakers Diane has been a newspaper, magazine, television, and radio journalist since 1991. She is currently completing a master's degree in Journalism. Over the years, she has traveled by train, ferry, seabus, horse-drawn carriage, sailboat, subway, streetcar, tractor, and canoe. She does not own a car and relies on public transit, carpooling, and her own two feet to get where she needs to go.